THE BOOK OF NAMES

NEW AND SELECTED POEMS

by

BARTON SUTTER

BOA EDITIONS, LTD. • BROCKPORT, NY • 1993

LC #: 92-73595
Cloth ISBN: 0-918526-96-5
Paper ISBN: 0-918526-97-3

2 3 4 5 6 7 8 9 0

The publication of books by BOA Editions Ltd. is made possible with the
assistance of grants from the Literature Program of the New York State
Council on the Arts and the Literature Program of the National
Endowment for the Arts, as well as from the Lannan Foundation,
and the Lila Wallace – Reader's Digest Literary Publishers Marketing
Development Program.

Cover Design: Daphne Poulin
Typesetting: Foerster FineLines, York Beach, ME
Manufacturing: McNaughton & Gunn, Lithographers
BOA Logo: Mirko

BOA Editions, Ltd.
A. Poulin, Jr., President
92 Park Avenue
Brockport, NY 14420

For Deb and Edith Wylder
seers and believers

Contents

New Poems

from CEDARHOME

DECLARATION OF DEPENDENCE

I write to avenge my mother's death.
I dreamed of becoming a woman
For my father's sake. I have become one.
My father remarried and left me
To fill the empty place
Beside her grave like a man.
I'm doing the best I can.

I write for Scandinavians
In English. I send off my poems
Like underwater cablegrams.
Asleep, Norwegian fishermen haul up their nets
Full of foreign fish they cannot name.

My words are food
I feed the tiny octopus
Sewn up in the sack I carry
Below the belt.

I am reciting the words
To make myself a prince
Who will kiss and wake
The beauties asleep in the woman
I have always loved.

If the moon is a woman
I write for the man in the moon.
I write for wind and rain
As if they could give a damn.

I write for the wolf and loon.
I am the poem
My dreams write
For the crows who cover me in my sleep.

I have nothing to do with it.
I am the dream
Daydreamed by immigrants.
My poems are my own
Crude translations.
I know I will never come true,
But this is what I have to do.

TALKING TO GRANDPA EASTMAN

What did you think, restless one?
Sex was artificial respiration?
While your wife stood by your daughter
And helped her die, you did your bit,
Chasing women as if life depended on it.
That daughter of yours was my mother.
Am I supposed to forgive you?

If it's any comfort, I haven't cried
Over her dead body, or yours, for years.
I know the sauna of sex can make a man
Come cleaner than confession, and how
For whipping up the blood, taboos
And guilt will do more than cedar boughs.
So how am I supposed to forgive you?

Forget it. Rest in peace,
Whiskey breath, wrestling partner,
Riveter of ships and women.
You held yourself together,
Called Christ a crutch, lived
And died for your own damned sins.
I won't dig up this dirt again.

LOVE POEM

Me on my back, you your front,
We sprawl out lazylike.
The smooth of your side looks cool
As milk in a metal pail.
Tastes a little like it, too.
Now that buttersoft, secret,
Sweet saltlick between your legs.
Now I lay me down on you.

WARMTH

Sometimes want makes touch too much.
I hold my hands over your body
Like someone come in from the cold
Who takes off his clothes
And holds out his hands to the stove.

I LOVE YOUR CRAZY BONES

Even your odds and ends.
I love your teeth, crazy bones,
Madcap knees and elbows.
Forearm and backhand
Hair makes you animal,
Rare among things.
The small of your back could pool rain
Into water a man might drink. Perfect,
From the whirlpools your fingers print
On everything you touch
To the moons on the nails of all ten toes
Rising and setting inside your shoes
Wherever you go.

DEATHWATCH

1.

This woman is nobody's woman.
She is dead. Rosaries are said.

The mortician, a run down wind-up toy,
The Monsignor, smooth as coffin silk:
These are good men, family friends.

The father has more grief than he knows
What to do with. He takes out his wallet
As if he could give it away.

Sisters survive her.
We who love them stand by,
Guilty with good luck. Careful.
As if each of us held a brimful
Water glass in both hands.

The widower is a black widow spider,
A bomb, a radioactive pile. No one goes near.
He stands, his hands holding each other,
Head bowed in a kind of shame,
Like someone left over after all
The sides have been chosen.

2.

Warming up in their truck,
The diggers wait.
They forgot to cover the backhoe tracks.

The casket has the blue-grey look
Of lakes in hunting weather.
We sing a song. The others leave.

My lover feels the coffin
Like a forehead for fever,
Finds no warmth, and weeps.
I am no comfort.

It's hard to leave the grave
To those who do
The lonely work they do with dirt.

3.

Friends find the family
Drawn up in a circle,
Dealing out cards and jokes.

A sister tells one on her sister.
"Laugh?" she laughs, "I like to died."
And then begins to cry.

I step outside.
The moon floats like ice
In a dark drink. Whatever
You're supposed to do with
Death is a mystery to me.

The hands on my wristwatch
Make a little phosphorescent
Checkmark in the dark.

NIGHT SHIFT: THE COMPOSING ROOM

They clock out and wait, worn out,
Too sick of words for words, a jumble
Of odd characters, shiftless night shift types:
The pianist famous for typewriter riffs,
The karate expert, the Armenian author,
The teetotaling nightclub singer,
The ex-con gone straight who still prefers to work at night,
The drunk so pie-eyed print rightside up looks upside down.

Shut-down. The fluorescent night light flutters,
A tropical moth in a killing jar. The linotypes—complicated,
Man-sized mousetraps—are all baited with manuscript.
The slugs and saws and presses are left to their own devices.
Repro proofs, displayed like choice cuts of meat, prove
These men are good for something.
The bright boil and buzz of machinery
Turned down to a glimmering hum,
The foreman puts the lid on it.

The crew crowds onto the lift, survivors on a life raft.
The author scrawls "Day shift eats it" on the wall
And gets a laugh. The elevator lets them down.
Good night. Good morning. Good night.

The Armenian rewrites the great Armenian novel in his sleep,
The blackbelt breaks gold bricks, the piano player
Turns into a player piano. The singer sweats in the spotlight
And scrabbles his lyrics, the drunk gets drunk
By something inky and bigger than he is.
The ex-con, caught in his nightmare,
Dreams he is sentenced to forty years of hard labor.
They shuffle the messy proof and try and try to justify
The same old ragged copy, the stories of their lives.

Meantime, it's morning, the dayside comes on.
They find the alphabets, letter by letter, in every case,
Bits of lead, distributed, like tools in well kept kits,
Rough-cut jewels they've inherited.

HOMING

The river whispers the way
My grandmother used to talk to herself.
I lean against a tree and listen.
When I open my eyes, my frozen
Breath waits in the air,
Ready to break into speech.

Ahead in the path, tattered birch bark:
Pages torn from a book.
I have forgotten
The language in which the story is written.

But I know the story by heart.
I shrug my shoulders, shift
The weight on my back.
My feet read the braille of the path
I follow. I know this story. It ends
In fire, food, all the old friends.

TRYING TO DREAM UP AN ANSWER

Like a compass needle
I keep coming back.
I can't explain the attraction,
Though I keep imagining this vein of ore
Turning to blood beneath a ridge
That would explain everything.

All morning, up to my neck in sunlight,
I have dozed in this clearing,
Trying to dream up an answer
To why I have come so far.
As if dreams told only the truth.
As if all these miles meant something.

NIGHT OUT

Ten p.m. Half lit, Lenny Benson
Roars up the highway,
Six-pack on the seat beside him.
He pounds the steering wheel, old friend,
The night has just begun.

Deer, driven out by haunch-high snow,
Crowd close to the road. Their eyes
Reflect headlights as well as anything
Put out by the highway men.

He stops at the Dew Drop Inn
For a quick one, picks up Diana.
The road is a frozen river.
Lenny fishtails all the way
To Thunder Bay and back.

Four a.m. The Dew Drop Inn's gone dark.
In the booth where she dropped, Diana
Dreams of another man.
And Lenny Benson, two parts drunk,
One part dream, one part Lenny Benson,
Slips in his chair, slips toward sleep, but fights it,
Aiming his empty beer glass like a flashlight
At the head of the dead wolf on the wall.

STALKING THE WILD MUSHROOM

Gourmet's roulette.
You need a guidebook
And lots of luck.

They are all in the same family:
Brothers to the frost
That jacks up the sidewalk,
Sisters to the terrible
Secrets of children.

They go up
Like tiny atomic bombs, something
Come near out of nothing
And going back again.
They must loom
Like water towers
To an ant, like shade trees
To a worm.

I find them
Beside an oxbow of old highway.
The freeway runs right by them,
Hissing like rain
In another world.

Those, disguised as clams,
Clinging to tree trunks
Like barnacles, are no good.
But these, tender, no bigger
Than the penises of three-year-olds,
Are good to eat. They feel
Much like the breasts of women.

I collect them. I take them home
And fry them alive. In the pan
They seem to complain
And I murmur something
Comforting,
Something like "Mushroom,
Mushroom." I can't wait.
I put one where my mouth is
And think of elves.

Don't laugh.
It's a serious business.
People have died.

CEDARHOME

1.

Make no mistake. The cedar
Is no weeping willow,
Has nothing to do
With women washing their hair.
What then? Hunchback? Gnome?
It isn't either. Whatever
Shape it assumes—peublo ladder
Leaning into the skylight,
Upright as fire, crouched over
Like some dumb oversized
Bird that migrated into the muck
Of the early paleozoic—
Its feathery leaves are evergreen.
Cedar is a survivor.

It takes root
And stays root,
Becoming whatever it clings to.
It likes lakes and rivulets,
Swamps and sloughs, the dark beer
And winesap of things
Seeping back to ground zero.
It sucks them up, it lifts them from nothing
Up to its crown and leaves them there.
It wants wet, but, lacking that,
Can pass as a cold country cactus,
A patient, camel kind of plant,
Survive on blasted granite switchbacks.
Cedar is sinewy, tougher than we are.

The way cedar trees
Smell makes me think
Of things I like to drink:

Wellwater, gin, after-the-rain jasmine tea.
They smell like star anise,
They smell like the sea.
They are none of these.
Cedar is a thing in itself.

2.

Just learning to talk, I watched
My father's father shiver cedar shakes,
Slit them to splinters
With a flick of his jackknife,
Shave off curls, auburn, blond,
To kindle kitchen stove and furnace.
My mother kept her wedding dress
In a cedar chest to stave off
Moth and rot. She trusted cedar
With special treasures.
My father taught me to know one
When I saw one.

Cedar must be my relative.
Around it, I turn primitive.
I take one for my totem.
Why not? The tree has a worthy history.
In paintings by Zen masters
They often appear, not quite there
In the mist. American Indians
Censed themselves with sage
And cedar. Swedes and Finns
Built saunas out of it
And whipped their wet bodies
Ruddy clean with greens of it.
Solomon beamed a temple
For the tribes of Israel
With the cedars of Lebanon.

3.

Can you believe it?
The Bible says: "Heaven
Lies north through the cedars."
I have doubted the word
But never the tree's
Fine facticity.

I once thought the twisted
Trunks perverted. And then one night
By firelight I saw the light:
The torque of the trunk tightens
In proportion to the persistence
With which it screws into muck and bedrock.
And the cedar's positive power
To retain and loose life after death
Proves, inversely,
The force of the process aforesaid,
Releasing, of course, the corollary:
To wit, death is only apparent,
Not nought.

How could I doubt it?
Hell, I was burning the evidence!
The deadfall I'd cut to the heart
Undid rivery ribbons of fire and smoke,
Streamers untwisting into the heavens.
What a warm, what an empirical proof!

The island I was on was adrift, a raft,
And the moon hung up
On a branch like a lantern. And then,
As if I needed a talking to,
A straggling line of geese,
A whole host of snows and blues,
Floated over, gaggling north.

4.

I didn't used to care much
What they did with me after I died.
Now I think I'd like to be planted
In a coffin knocked out of cedar planks.
What sweet seasoning that would be,
What a sloughing of flesh, what a mulch,
What peat-rich mouldering,
What lingering commingling,
What a cedarhome.

WHAT THE COUNTRY MAN KNOWS BY HEART

1.

Why he lives there he can't say.
Silence is the rule.

But he knows where to look
When his wife is lost. He knows
Where the fish that get away go
And how to bring them back.
He's learned about lures
And knows how deep the bottom is.

He has been lost and found
Where he lives moss grows everywhere.
He's made his way home
The way gulls fly through fog,
Find where water turns to stone.

In country covered with trees
He can find the heartwood
That burns best.
He can find his wife in smoke.

2.

When loons laugh he does not;
He waits for what follows,
Feeling the meaning of animal speech
Crawl in the base of his brain.

But he knows there are no words
To answer the question the owl has kept
Asking all these years.

He knows a man alone
Will begin to talk to himself
And why at last he begins to answer.

3.

He would never say any of this.
He knows how often silence speaks
Better than words; he knows
Not to try to say as much.

But then he won't say either
How often he longs to break the rule,
How unspoken words writhe in his throat
And blood beats the walls of his heart.

DAYBREAK

A goldeneye whistles across the lake
And the dream breaks. I get up;
I go outside to see what's up.

It's one of those mornings.
No matter how softly I step,
I knock lichens off their perches,
Birds and animals disappear.

I walk to the water's edge and kneel,
Drink cold handfuls of my reflection.
When I am done, I am still there.

from

PINE CREEK PARISH HALL AND OTHER POEMS

PINE CREEK PARISH HALL

If what we remember is what we are,
Then I'm the Pine Creek Parish Hall.
Who was that guy who played guitar
And testified there when I was small?

Wasn't it Gust? Gust Nordvall.
I believed everything. Jesus.
Today I doubt that I could recall
The creed if I tried. The place is

All that remains of my old-time religion:
Nameless faces, folding chairs,
A poorly converted pioneer cabin.
My dreams will often take me there,

And just as I enter, the music starts.
Those farmers who sneered at factory wages
Bellow the hymns they know by heart:
The Old Rugged Cross and Rock of Ages.

GENEVA

She was famous for kindness, Geneva.
And yet she could run down a hen
And chop off its head just like that.
"Macaroni!" I said, when I saw the insides,
And she crowed like a satisfied rooster.
I once watched her husband, the only man
I knew who had a mustache, string up
And slaughter a cow. I ran to Geneva
And buried my face in her lap. "Geneva,"
I said, "does it hurt?" "That old cow?"
Said Geneva. "Don't worry," she said.
"You don't feel a thing when you're dead."

Geneva giggled and taught me to piss
In the dark in a thunder jug.
I was from town and embarrassed,
But Geneva enjoyed that noise.
She taught me itchweed and outhouse.
She spanked me and wiped my ass.
She was a good one, Geneva.
The world was a joke, and everyone said:
"She's a real card, that Geneva."

She had warts and a nose, Geneva,
And a twisted smile with teeth,
But she also had beautiful daughters.
Hay and fresh faces and breasts.
They could cook. The kitchen had pails,
And everyone drank from the dipper.
I can taste the tang of the tin
And smell that slop-bucket stink
And the fragrance of bread on the table.
She was always baking, Geneva.

She taught me the stars, Geneva.
It was night. In the garden.
She was giving us something again:
Carrots, cucumbers, tomatoes, and such,
Everything cool and slick. "Chicken shit,"
Said Geneva. "That's the secret," she said.
My pants were all wet with the dew.
"Look at that," said Geneva
And showed me the star-spangled sky.
"It's a coloring book," said Geneva.
"It's all dot-to-dot. Don't you see?"
And I saw: The Sisters, The Hunter,
The Bull and the Bear, The Dipper
From which we all drank.

So I thank the stars for Geneva,
All of her muscles and fat, that
Quick chicken-killer, that ugly
She of the beautiful daughters
And prize-winning hogs, that woman
Of pickles and jam. Geneva,
She taught me the mud and the stars,
And when I am ready to die
She will come with her hatchet in hand
And her face like a kerosene lamp
And her dress all feathers and blood.

THE BEAVERHOUSE DOWNRIVER

In the old forever-never days
When I was blond and ten,
A beaver clan claimed the bend
Across the river. They badgered holes
And rumpus room, adobe dens
And chimney flues, spiral ramps and hatchways:
A complex, subterranean terrarium.
They chiselled and chewed
Through cottonwoods and poplars
As thick as cabin logs. With simple, secret
Principles of beaver mathematics,
They muscled timber down the bank
And built a barricade, an earthwork
Battlement of naked sticks
Plastered up and stuccoed
With pungent rivermuck.
They made the water sleep.
They littered the river with bittersweet
Aspen, alder, elder, willow
Chips and leaves and strips of juicy bark.

Behind a blind of willow slash,
The Wetzler boys and I stood watch
Until the trees grew together
And the early evening floodlight failed.
Then we caterwauled applause
That the beavers would return
With their crackshot tails.
We watched with sympathy half animal.
Full of the devil, there were days
We downed a tree ten times our age,
Lopped off limbs, bucked the trunk,
And peeled the green bark back
For fun, for no good reason

But the slippery feel of slick sapwood.
We were builders, too—constructed
Huts and forts and lean-to's, dugouts
To protect us from our enemies, adults,
Who owned the world.
Everything the beavers did
They did without the help of men.
And so we loved them,
Savagely. Jimmy trapped one
With a steel-jaw, an underwater set
He'd read about. I forget
The fur, the teeth I should remember.
The tail was a thick, tough tongue—
Rough and cold, reptilian.
We talked of mountain men
Who ate them, and, after a day or two,
We threw the beaver back
In the black river where it belonged.

By late fall the moat froze.
We attacked the dam, pried loose
Dry deadwood, built bonfires.
Up to no good one day, we were
Nosing around their animal manholes
When something cracked
And Ken fell in.
We thought they'd kill him.
A crow cawed twice. Under ice,
The river groaned.
Then Ken called out: "Come on!
Nobody's home!"

Down under: dark and warm,
The quiet of a country church,
A bombshelter without the war.
It was peaceful as a pantry, a cellar
Stocked with sedge and arrowhead,

Roots and tubers, baby potatoes, wild onion.
The floor had Oriental rugs:
Scattered mats of cattail, rush and reed.
There was sitting room, a sleeping ledge,
Nooks where we could range
Our pocket knives and precious stones.
And did. It was complicated,
The way we felt down there.

We went there daily. That hideaway
Was just what we wanted,
A wild retreat where we were free
To practice our religion:
Tobacco and women.
The smoke inspired angry guesses.
What were they, under their dresses?
Tits were tits, of course, but
Was it really gunt or was it cunt?
And was it true about the hair?
And did your father ever
Kiss your mother there?
Such talk. But mostly we just sat
Scared quiet, half-ecstatic, expecting
Some she-beaver to come
Barreling out of a burrow,
Terrible as a grizzly bear,
As good as God.

What happened? We never
Saw the beavers again.
Later a construction gang
Straightened out the river,
And, boys, we couldn't help it,
We kept on getting bigger,
And we moved away forever,
And all the grown-ups died.

THE VISITOR

The man whose muscles I once admired
Answers my knock with a vague smile,
Sure I'm a stranger who's made a mistake.
My name brings a laugh and a handshake.
He draws me in, calling his wife to the kitchen.
Mary, once mysterious and thin,
Has thickened. And John, the man
Whose boys would hightail it home
Like a pair of buckshot pups
When he whistled them to supper,
This man's giving way to gravity.
He slumps. He's grey.
Something broke and gentled him.
I like him even more than I did then.
A jug of honey heats on the stove,
The crystals turning to liquid amber
While the coffeepot mutters
And we discuss the Andersons' daughter,
Who died of what and who
Gave up and why they moved,
Which old bat had it coming,
Who went to jail, who made a killing,
Who loved who and had a bastard,
Small-town triumphs, personal disasters.

And after the coffee and strawberries
I say my goodbyes to Mary
And troll the large lawn with John,
Fishing for memories and finding these
Fruits of his faith: two maple trees,
Willowy and weak when we were young,
Casting astonishing clouds of shade.
I imagine autumn, see red,
And we talk of his apples and cherries.

I tell him how many young people
Would envy the place that he's made.
He's proud, but he says that it's simple.
"Just plant and stay put. Things grow."
Myself, I can dream up a harvest
And even imagine a moment in winter, with frost
Like a frieze on the windows,
When you're snug and sit back and smile
At the red-and-white bite in the apple.
But where do you get the patience, the faith?
My life's more like water than trees.
We inspect his boxes of bees,
And the air grows thick with the hum
Of the engine of work and belief.

I have to run. John hands me a gift
Through the window. I hit the gas
And I'm gone. The town belongs to Mary and John
And the friendly strangers who wave as I pass.
I see that old abandoned place
The Nelsons rebuilt is abandoned again.
The engine drones. I shift and slow
For the curve that threw
A carload of kids twenty years ago.
I feel the same centrifugal tug,
But I'm out of the curve and over the hill,
The landscape reeling while the car stands still.
I steady the needle at sixty
And glance at the gift on the carseat
Beside me: a glowing hunk of honeycomb
The bees in their language of legs called home.
Tonight, in my room in the city,
I will sample those delicate spaces
And imagine other lives, other places.

SWEDISH LESSON

Talk about the mother tongue.
I heard these words when I was young.
I'd gabble gibberish and stutter,
Mimicking my babysitters.
They'd say, "Can you speak svenska?"
I'd answer, "Ya, you betcha."
They'd giggle, slap their laps, and sigh.
Their gossip was my lullabye.
Around the barn their men would grunt
The Esperanto of immigrants.

My grandmother risked ridicule
Whenever she opened her mouth at school
But broke the brogue. I speak American,
But, feeling like a bad translation,
I bought the books and paid tuition.
My classmates mock my pronunciation.

Once these words were hawked and spit
By barbarians who meant it
When they swore. They drew swords
And mangled men for what they said.
These words are theirs but tamed by time,
Their history a wind chime.
Hearsay now, they sound so gentle
I think of women spinning wool.
Chuckling like a dandling song,
The melodic nonsense passes on
Rumors of the old country. We
Hear the schuss of snow and ski
Past places parents mentioned.
Strange. The teacher's intonation
Makes every other word a question.

Blue-collar misfits, dissatisfied
Housewives, we've stood beside
Our ancestors, laid hands on headstones,
Wondering why they ever left home,
Mystified by the rotten spoils
Of the Viking dream of silk and jewels.
We've traced the foreign, familiar names
Chiselled in grim cuneiform.
The rune stones resist interpretation.

And so we've begun this reverse migration.
God knows what we hope to learn.
The motives of the arctic tern?
We murmur, uncertain what we're about,
But, counting together, we launch the boat.
I swear by my grandmother's face
And steer to the north, northeast.
I stammer and repeat my faith
In the dead, their hope, their anguish,
Buried alive in this, their language.

REAL ESTATE

The orchard's gorgeous,
And the dirt looks expensive as coal.
But the house, rank with the odor of moldy hay,
The walls all riddled with daylight,
Hardly calls up happy nights.
Still, the barn's all right, and there's the pond.
The couple who worked this place, they say,
Weren't the kind you asked to dinner.
She liked boys, and he, so gossip has it,
Had his animals in revenge.
Between them they drank up three farms
And died in debt. And yet
Those oaks grew straight,
And the neighbors made a bundle on hay
Here just last year. Was it winters, isolated,
Made them hate each other so? God knows,
Hating weather never paid the high return
Hurting some one person does.
The weather played hell
With that old windmill.
Loves me, loves me not.
Half the blades are broken off;
The blossom droops on the stalk.
But the fencerow's full of pheasants.
The hunting should be good.
This braided wire borders the place
And gives a point to abstract terms
Like trespassing and property.
Barbed as a rose bush,
Tough as a grape vine,
Twisted round and round itself
Like the runners that grow morning glories.
But all man-made. Blossomless.
It came unstrung right here, I guess.

What's this? Why, this
Wire never was unwound,
Just rusted to this reddish brown
And kept the coiled shape it had
When she or he who carried it laid down
This wreath of nettles,
This metal crown of thorns.

HUSBANDRY

And what does the farmer's daughter think,
Scrubbing tit-cups at the stainless steel sink?
What does she think while she bottle-feeds
The calf that sucks with such desperate need?
Does she wonder about her new breasts
Of which she's both proud and embarrassed?
What does she think when she tugs at a tit
And the milk so warm, so runny and wet?

She's thinking mainly about the money
Tonight's milking will bring. She worries
About the smell of her hair, though it's trapped
Beneath a day-glo hunting cap. She sways
With pails that feel warm as stove-pipe
And pours them steaming into the bulk tank.
She turns the herd loose and heads for the house,
Stopping halfway for the hunter's moon.
If she has a secret, that's what she thinks
While she stands in dry leaves like a dress at her feet.

Now for a shower and lots of shampoo.
They say such awful things at school.
She enters the living room wrapped in her robe,
And her father asks, "How did it go?"
"I'm afraid Penelope's got pink-eye."
"Good girl," he says. "I'll go check."
She thinks how her dad has grown kind of shy,
How he won't tease her the way he once did.
She thinks of school and what the kids said
And how she darn near died. She thinks of the sweet,
Sour smell of cowhide and then
Piles her hair in a terry-cloth turban.
A few strands leak out over her cheek.
She hugs herself and thinks of her father,

His rough-and-ready gentleness,
His huge hands, their calluses.
She moves over close to the coal-oil burner
And thinks: "When I marry, I'll marry a farmer."

THE SMALL WHITE FLOWER THAT
CONTAINS THE SUN

I shuffle through the leaves of the worn out woods.
Birds reinterpret the classical songs,
The tough old trees are beaded with buds,
And the path is spiked with three green prongs.
Having noticed these, I see many more
Protruding from the trash of the forest floor.

Curious, I kneel and examine one.
The odd green thumb is really a sheaf
That hides the bud concealing the pollen.
Stripped of the soft, leathery leaf,
The petals appear. White and quite tender,
They depend on a dab of bright butter.

I can't recall their proper name.
I'd say daisies if they weren't so small.
Oh, well. They don't know who I am
Either. Call me the shadow that smells
And this force, so free of ambition,
The small white flower that contains the sun.

They do not remind me of women,
Although they're impressively sexy,
But of something asleep within men.
The petals feel damp and waxy.
In the distance, a single partridge drums,
And the squirming frog pond thrums.

THE STALLION

Walking the dry winter woods,
I reached the hidden pasture
And paused to admire the mare and stud
Till he came after me, the bastard.

He ran right at me, reared,
And whipped around to kick.
I hollered, "Hyah!" but he didn't hear,
So I retreated, throwing sticks.

He'd always been shy and mild,
But the mare was so fat with his foal
He'd suddenly grown wild,
Proud as a prince, powerful.

He chased me half a mile
Till I rolled beneath a fence.
He stood there sweating, male,
Magnificent. I dusted off my pants.

"So long," I said, "you son of a bitch."
And headed home. The sky was red and violet.
Reeds and cattails rattled in the ditch.
I felt a wonderful violence.

OLD MRS. COURT AND HER QUILT

She is Raggedy Ann at seventy-six,
And her arthritic hands do astonishing tricks.
Refusing to hobble her thumb with a thimble,
She has to put up with some painful pricks,

But her fingers, surprisingly nimble,
Make the intricate piecework seem simple.
They flutter and smooth and stitch up the quilt
That's come to consume the whole kitchen table.

Patches of cotton, triangles of felt,
The traditional plaid of a Highland kilt,
A great big bite out of somebody's pants
Are seen, assembled, and sewn with skill.

"My hobby," she says, "is collecting remnants."
While watching her wrinkled fingers dance,
We know there's a goddess, a great grandmother
Who defeats wear and tear, chaos, and chance.

For this cloak, so carefully gathered together
From tatters and strips of so many colors,
Will seem to say to the couple it covers:
Though your lives are in pieces, love one another.

WITCH TREE

Grown out of granite,
She's cut like a bowsprit

Through flurries of snow, fog, spray,
And simmering midsummer days.

She must take her moisture
Out of the air. There's no humus here—

Only a few fluorescent
Lichens that grow on the rock like rust.

Resisting the seasonal seesaw,
This tree supports ephemera.

At the moment, a fritillary butterfly
Flickers around the roots, and high

Up the trunk a spider suspends a net,
A doily both deadly and delicate,

To fish for flies. This driftwood
Lives and, most lately, has withstood

Picture postcards, stupid verses,
Chippewa legends, the Chamber of Commerce.

So far, no vandals have dared
To carve initials here.

So God bless fear and superstition,
Whatever grants this tree protection.

They say she's a witch,
But she burns like a blowtorch,

Inhales the breath of animals,
Converts exhausted air to chlorophyl,

Gives off the oxygen
We breathe, and it begins again.

Biology may call this photosynthesis,
But, sitting here, I know that this is

Grandma, old and gnarled.
This is the light of the world.

THE SNOWMAN

This is a poem for Tom.
This is a poem for Tom Blair.
This is a poem for him
And for all of the men on the edge
Of their beds in their underwear,
Wondering what they're doing there.
This is a poem for them.
For all of the good providers.

The place of the poem is Chicago.
The time of the poem is the great snow
Of nineteen hundred and seventy-nine.
In '79 it snowed so that
People fought over parking spots.
Arms were twisted, headlights busted.
And all because of the snow.
Not that I blame the snow.
No, the snow was only the weather.
I'm talking about something else altogether.

Thomas Blair drove a plow,
And because of the snow in '79
He worked a lot of overtime.
Not that I blame the snow.
But because of the snow
The work was there,
And there was the wife and kid,
A regular blizzard of debts, and so
The food of the poem is coffee,
Coffee and cigarettes.

Tom went to work,
And he worked and worked,
With little time off,

And he worked and worked,
And one day, Tom,
He went berserk.
He forgot all about the snow
And started plowing up cars,
And some had people in them,
And some of the people died.

Can you see the blue lights of his truck?
The cherrytops of the cops?
He wrecked forty cars with the plow
Before they got him stopped,
And when they could hear
What the screaming said,
You know what the screaming said?
"I hate my job!
I want to see my kid!
I hate my goddamned job!"

So that's it. That's the poem.
What do you think?
What do you think it's all about?
It's not about the snow
So much as . . . I'll tell you
What it's about.
This is a poem for Tom.
This is a poem for Tom Blair.
This is a poem for him
And for all of the men on the edge
Of their beds in their underwear,
Wondering what they're doing there.
This is a poem for them.
For all of the good providers.

A GOOD NIGHT

for Ross

My brother sighs in his sleep,
And the springs of the rollaway squeak.
Another ne'er-do-well. What a family!
Troubadours and dreamers. Nobody has any money.
I'm sitting up with a glass of wine,
Staring through the tattered blind,
Strung out from work, trying to kill
My nerves with the last dose of alcohol
In the house.
                    Suddenly
Light blooms in a window across the way:
A woman, nursing her baby, sways
In the frame, and a cat sits on the sill.
Quiet. Even the leaves are still.
Dear woman, I see you. Temporarily,
I love you ... and your hungry kid ...
And your cat like a silhouette ...
And I hate cats.
                    The cat
Drops out of the window, the window
Goes blank, then black. It's 3 a.m.,
And here I am, in the midst of my life,
And already I miss it.
                    Good night.

HALLOWEEN ON HENNEPIN

It's Halloween going on midnight. Boo.
So what's happening? The usual Hennepin Avenue
Sideshow, only more so: a parade
Of pimps in costumes custom-made
With sequins, studs, and stars enough
To knock your eye out; renegade Sioux;
A few blue policemen; a dwarf
Or two for good measure;
Roughnecks on every corner;
A regular cakewalk of whores.
What you see is what you get
For naming streets after Jesuits.
Poor old Father Hennepin.
He thought the Indians were pagan.
If he knew how his namesake needs him,
He'd come back to haunt the heathen.
And maybe he's here, for Christ's sake.
A queer, forgiving attitude
Mingles with the fumes on the avenue
Tonight. The usual goofballs don't seem sick.
This fag in drag, for instance, skirt slit
Up to the crotch, silk shirt
Pregnant with foam rubber knockers.
Hobbled by heels that have to hurt,
He can hardly walk. He does an imitation,
A drunken, awkward, hippety hopscotch
That draws applause from streetwalkers.
Still, the mockery has limitations.
If you want to be your sister,
It's okay, Mister. We'd rather
Be someone else, ourselves. And those of us
Coming off nightshift, going on graveyard,
Plainclothes people, waiting for the bus,
Take a different attitude

Toward the prostitutes tonight.
What the hell? We're all co-workers.
When a hooker with a puss
Like a jack-o-lantern offers,
"Hello, Luv." I answer,
And we chat about the weather
And the costumes until she pushes off.
People returning from parties pass
For Frankenstein and Dracula,
A horse's head and a horse's ass,
A pretty pair of nuns.
The guy beside me asks,
"What's black and white
And black and white and black and white?"
"A nun falling down stairs," I laugh.
"Everyone knows that one."
Finally our coach arrives,
And the stumblebums with shopping bags,
Hungry bachelors, working wives,
All board. Soon the doors flap open
For the hobbledehoy with plastic legs
And aluminum sticks, who lugs
Himself around by hand
Like a broken-backed amphibian.
The biddy ahead of me meows,
"Poor soul," as always,
And looks away out the window.
A nurse gets up to leave and sways
Like laundry on the line. The burgundy blot
She wears across her heart
Is not a carnation. Tomorrow
I'll be more than half afraid
Of this grim carnival,
This motley masquerade.
All this fellow feeling will sour
Into lonesome fury, sure
As I'll be sitting here. Now, though,

I'm confused by affection.
Spooky. Almost Christian.
Not knowing exactly what I mean,
I say to the stranger beside me,
"Hey. Happy Halloween."

NOVEMBER 7, 1984

Not one of my candidates won. Not one.
So I go for a walk in the woods,
Where I've gone for help since childhood.
Here you can howl like a wounded wolf
Or suck the slick bones of defeat
And who cares? Blasted tree trunks
And fallen limbs, ruin all around me,
Say, "Hey. It's a familiar story."
The leaves lie fading like wet confetti,
Like crepe paper streamers and broken balloons.

The lady who lives downstairs—
A tough old girl who farmed for years
And used to slaughter—wept last night.
"I must be getting old," she apologized.
"But if Reagan's elected you might as well croak.
That's just how I feel." I felt numb.
She'd used up all the grief in the room,
So I took what was left and swore
And stomped and slammed some doors
While my wife sat still, struck dumb.

Now there's the scent of snow on the wind.
Crows boil up out of the oaks
Like smoke from a fire of rubber tires.
Sundown. Dark. I turn for home.
Home, I pour a few fingers of whiskey
And flick on the lights. Burn, baby, burn.
I've got a sizeable chip on my shoulder
And a cocklebur stuck to my collar
Like a political pin. My socks and sleeves
Bristle with stickers and seeds.

A CELEBRATION OF RUST

I am so weak my enemies
Have never even heard of me.
And even if they knew me, even if
I crashed their party,
They would smile on me
With contemptuous courtesy
While the goblets in their hands
Glittered like teeth. I speak
Of the take-charge guys,
The ones who own all the neckties,
And the women who wish they were men.

They don't even know who I am.
And why should they? I am
Nothing much, myself, so much dust,
But I do have powerful friends.
Termites, for instance, and ants,
The soft emery cloth of the wind,
Sandpaper snowstorms, and rain,
The mild acids of which
Will eventually etch their names
Off all the monuments
And melt down every memorial.

I have many powerful friends.
Frost may be my favorite,
But rust is one of the best
And the truest. Rust is the breath
That clouds the full-length mirror where
The men made of money admire themselves.
It takes years, but it will attack
Airplanes and tanks, banks and bridges
With equal indifference and win.

I take great satisfaction in rust.
It is patience in action
And powerful as the grass. Rain
Runs a bead which is welded by sunlight,
And red soot reduces blue steel
To a powder. A mineral amoeba,
Rust eats iron and multiplies
As furiously as a fungus. It deepens
Like humus, collecting and building
A fine film of metallic dust.

This is raw power. This is the cutting edge
Between here and there. It borders on air
And will finish the shiniest surface.
And when the buildings of the high and mighty
Have finally fallen and rest in ruins,
They will be blanketed with dried blood,
With rust, the loveliest pollen.

TOOLS

1.

My dad's old man was a carpenter
Who could build a coffin or cabinet,
Whatever the customer called for.
The latches clicked. The lid fit.

But during the Great Depression
He ran out of work and luck.
Nobody asked for craftsmen.
It got tough to turn a buck.

He heard there was work in Oklahoma,
And, tired of fussing around the place
And feeling less and less at home,
He packed his tools and an old suitcase.

Seek, the Good Book said,
And you shall surely find.
Grampa believed but also doubted
God ever had to stand in line.

Finally, one afternoon,
Or so the family story goes,
Half a dozen hungry men
Reported in sort of a row.

"Let's have a look at your tools,"
The foreman said. He had to choose.
Grampa's were filed, slick with oil,
Obviously used.

Meanwhile, back at the farm,
Everyone sat tight.
They hoped he hadn't come to harm
But wondered why he didn't write.

The pantry was all but empty
When the envelope arrived. "Dear Family,
Thought 'y'all' might like to see
Some of this Oklahoma money."

2.

As a boy my father preached to trees,
An imitation Lincoln.
I don't doubt the story's true.
I've heard the old man thinking.
Anyone so shy of speech
Had to teach himself to preach,
Rehearsing his religion
Until the leaves believed in sin.

The colorful stoles my father wore
Were covered with delicate braid.
Though his parishes were always poor,
His robes were all handmade.
His voice could make a sermon stick.
Whenever he went to see the sick
He carried a pocket communion kit
I covet and hope to inherit.

To see him fumble around the house,
You'd swear he'd lost his father's skill.
His hands were free of calluses,
But he could handle a funeral
So you'd believe in resurrection.
When he raised a hand in benediction
The peace that he pronounced was real.
Survivors felt their sorrow heal.

3.

The motto above my table says,
"Writers work with their hands."
Writing is really all in the wrist,
Not what you think you understand.

The way I thumb the dictionary
I could be ordering parts.
Syllables get ornery.
One word stops. Another starts.

An old-fashioned fountain pen
Seems to help my fingers think.
I like a nice twenty-pound bond
And permanent jet black ink.

SHOE SHOP

I shut the door on the racket
Of rush hour traffic,
Inhale the earthy, thick
Perfume of leather and pipe tobacco.

The place might be a barbershop
Where the air gets lathered with gossip.
You can almost hear the whippersnap
Of the straightedge on the razor strop.

It might be a front for agitators,
But there's no back room. A rabble
Of boots and shoes lies tumbled
In heaps like a hoard of potatoes.

The cobbler, broad as a blacksmith,
Turns a shoe over his pommel,
Pummels the sole, takes the nail
He's bit between his teeth

And drives it into the heel. Hunched
At his workbench, he pays the old shoe
More attention than me. "Help you?"
He grunts, as if the man held a grudge

Against business. He gives my run-over
Loafer a look. "Plastic," he spits.
"And foreign-made. Doubt I can fix it."
I could be holding a dead gopher.

"The Europeans might make good shoes,
But I never see them. Cut the price.
Advertise! Never mind the merchandise.
You buy yourself a pair, brand new,

"The welt will be cardboard
Where it ought to be leather.
There's nothing to hold the shoe together."
He stows my pair in a cupboard.

"And all of them tan with acid.
The Mexicans make fancy boots, but they cure
Their leather in cow manure. Wear
Them out in the rain once. Rancid?

"I had a guy bring me a pair.
Wanted me to get rid of the stink.
Honest to God. I hate to think
My customers are crazy, but I swear."

He curses factories, inflation,
And I welcome the glow of conspiracy.
Together we plot, half seriously,
A counter industrial revolution.

His pride's been steeped in bitterness,
His politics tanned with elbow-grease.
To hear him fume and bitch, you'd guess
His guerrilla warfare's hopeless.

But talk about job satisfaction!
To take a tack from a tight-lipped smile,
Stick it like a thorn in an unworn sole,
To heft the hammer, and whack it!

When I step back out in the street
The city looks flimsy as a movie set.

STATIC

Well, Old Flame, the fire's out.
I miss you most at the laundromat.
Folding sheets is awkward work
Without your help. My nip and tuck
Can't quite replace your hands,
And I miss that odd square dance
We did. Still, I'm glad to do without
Those gaudy arguments that wore us out.
I've gone over them so often
They've turned grey. You fade and soften
Like the hackles of my favorite winter shirt.
You've been a hard habit to break, Old Heart.
When I feel for you beside me in the dark,
The blankets crackle with bright blue sparks.

THE MAN SELLING PENCILS OUTSIDE THE B. DALTON BOOKSTORE

I blink, but there he sits, unreal
As an organ grinder or a breadline
In some jerky thirties newsreel.
I thought we had schools for the blind.

His cane looks like a stick of chalk,
But he advertises Pencils, 10 Cents.
The shoppers balk. Some stop to gawk.
I wonder if he has a license.

He's creating a disturbance,
But he's oblivious or bored.
He squats there like a dunce
Staring at the blackboard.

I've heard that some can see you
As a shadow or a silhouette
And others make out curlicues
And figure-eights of light.

So maybe he envisions patterns
Like meiosis, weird and lovely,
Like the spiral tracks of protons,
None of us can see.

The window at his back displays
Books no one would read in braille.
The fountain gurgles. Muzak plays.
And he offers pencils for sale.

Some of us buy. Just for kicks.
They don't cost much.
And none of us exist
Unless we speak, until we touch.

NORDEAST

We thought we'd try the new saloons
Thrown up along the river, and there,
As elegant as moonshine on the water
Or the fantasies of Scott Fitzgerald,
Sat the smart set of our generation:
Trim, tan, dressed in clothing so expensive
We could read the labels on their sleeves.
They looked like ads for happiness.
Doctors, we figured. Lawyers, we guessed.
Or maybe clerks in clothing stores.
Whoever they were, they were handsomely bored
And waiting to be noticed. Having seen enough,
We downed our high-priced drinks and left

And stopped at a nearby neighborhood bar
To drink in the exotic atmosphere
Of Slavic accents; vulgar jokes;
Loud, free laughter; thick, blue smoke.
Though the two of us were tourists
There, a stranger bought us each a beer.
And then the fat lady took the stage
And strapped an accordion across her chest.
Two old geeks about her age
Backed her with a sour saxophone
And a set of enthusiastic drums.
Nothing fancy about those tunes—
Old-time polkas, American schmaltz.
The bartender whistled and started to waltz,
And the shoes of the dancers were loaded with springs.
Had we ever felt any less alone?
Women led women onto the floor.
A man moved lightly in a pair of work boots.
Had anyone anywhere ever been bored?
A grey-haired couple kissed in a booth,

And a guy with a face that made us wince
Flirted with astonishing confidence.
Everyone everywhere seemed to be singing,
And we felt the place, like an airplane, lifting.
For the life of me, I could not quit grinning,
And my heart, that helpless squeeze box,
Kept repeating the same obnoxious
Oom-pah-pah of happiness.

HOARFROST AND FOG

I walk six blocks to the park.
Hoarfrost and fog and ten below zero,
A full twelve inches of snow.
No one believes in the mysteries
Anymore, but still, once or twice
Every year this will happen:
Hoarfrost and fog and snow all at once.
I don't often notice my breath,
But here I am breathing and breathing.
And here is a kid in a scarlet parka,
Pulling a sled through the sugarbush.
He knew all along this would happen.
I forget, and yet once, maybe twice a year,
We enter this other kingdom. We're here.
And here is a woman so black
And slender and thin, I think of a statue
My friend brought back from Liberia.
She is wading around with a camera,
As if she could capture this hoarfrost
And fog that is softer than breath.
We smile. She hesitates, then decides
She will speak. She says, "Oh!
In my country where I come from
We have many amazing things,
But there there is nothing like this!
I would like you if you take my picture?"
I fiddle with the little black box,
Back off, watch her smile and say,
"Can you fit all this everything
Inside the picture? Do you think it will show?"
"I don't know," I tell her. "I'll try."
My fingers are cold. The shutter is stiff,
But it clicks. The fruit tree behind her
Is heavy with frost, the apples are withered

But red. There is fog in the background,
The snow is nearly up to her knees.
I breathe, and I breathe, and I breathe.

LOST IN *ANTARCTICA*

If hell is hot, this must be heaven.
A mystic might have such a vision
Nearing death. These aren't pictures
Of the moon, Neptune, or Jupiter.
This is earth, and it is strange.
On every page I'm rearranged
By the view that Porter's chosen
And alchemically flash-frozen.

This is so far south of south
Every vantage point looks north.
The aerial shots cause vertigo.
I keep confusing rock with snow.
The ocean steams like smelting ore,
And the rubber seals along the shore
Are nothing compared to the penguins,
Which are birds but do not fly but swim.

This desert is home to animals
Who've somehow evolved without us,
Who live off the fat of the sea
And a couple of vague ideas.
Do they appreciate the sculpture
Everywhere, this rainbow-colored
Ice? Who knows? I suppose
They enjoy the way the wind blows.

A photograph of half a dog
Illustrates the gruesome logs
Of men who first explored this place
Like aliens from outer space.
The camera caught their biscuit cans
And oddly beautiful pots and pans.
In Shackleton's hut there's a frozen lunch
And a row of boots on a blue bench.

Porter took these in his seventies,
Transcending praise and envy.
The light looks hard as rock. This man
Braved the terrifying feminine
Force of water, snow, and loved it.
Here, and here again, we have it.
This is what it's like to earn your death,
To squint one eye and see the truth.

SKY

On a bright blue day in October
I go visit Grandma, who is so old
Her skin looks like *lefse*. She is half bald
But hardly unhappy. Air-conditioning, color TV,
More than enough money saved
To purchase her coffin,
A stone for the grave....
She says that she's never had it so good.
She pours the bitter, eternal coffee,
And, in one of her goofier moods,
Introduces the homemade cookies
By singing a little song about sweets
And how they make you thick and fat.
Her voice is thin and scratchy,
Like a worn-out 78.
At her age, eighty-seven,
She ought to be thinking of heaven,
But she tells me an off-color story
And warms the room with laughter.
Once again I ask her
The secret of her longevity.
Once again she tells me:
"Just keep breathing."

She has outlived everyone,
Surviving her husband,
Her family, and friends, and known
The final revenge of outlasting
All of her enemies. She is almost free
Of desire. Through her highrise window
I can see the topmost twigs of two trees
And the sky that simply goes and goes.
I think her mind must be like that
Or like some windswept pasture.

"It's the strangest feeling, Barton,
When all your friends are gone.
Dunc is dead. Myrtle is dead. And Verlie. Everyone
I grew up with, and we used to have such fun!"

I leave her alone, still hanging on,
A tough leaf the wind left behind,
And, driving home, I'm oddly excited
By the horses grazing the green hillsides
And the velvet cattails lining the road,
The scepters that rule the other kingdom,
And the certainty that a day will come
When I, too, will get to be old and die,
And I notice the brassy aspens,
And the birches are shining like brandy,
And the lakes look as deep as the sky.

New Poems

THE THIRD USE OF THE PENIS

My friend Ann, the reference librarian,
Sits at her desk like the goddess of knowledge,
And people come to her—regular people
And people in raincoats, people in turbans
And some with shaved heads, the kid
With his suitcase of dead radios,
The girl with the cue stick, people who smell bad,
People who can't remember their own last names,
People who tremble and stammer, people
Who haven't slept in six weeks—the people,
Yes, the people come. But Ann is no goddess
But rather a regular woman with breasts
And an excellent head for crosswords and Scrabble.
She is unbelievably brave. For the people, they come,
The troubled ones. They ask her things.
It's frightening.

Oh, some of them are easy ones, some of them are nothing.
She could answer them in her sleep, and she does.
How long is the longest river? Ho-hum.
How deep is the deepest lake? How many
Miles from here to the moon? Why are there stars?
What are the seven names of Jehovah? Excuse me,
But where is the bathroom?

But then there are those who have lost their way.
The boy with the briefcase and pocket of pens:
"Do you have any plans for atomic bombs?"
The woman so ashamed she blushes and sweats
And insists on writing her question down:
"What is a black belt in karate?" And who could forget
The man from City Hall who called to demand:
"Say, what century are we in?" These are the screwloose,
The scary, the ding-dongs, the very dangerous ones

On whom the future of the world depends.
Even these, very often, Ann is able to answer.

But one time she was completely stumped.
A middle-aged woman in a pink pants-suit
Inquired discreetly: "Can you tell me, please,
What is the third use of the penis?" Ann thought
Quite quickly of two, but the third?
Befuddled, she sent the woman away.
Research yielded no answer. Ann laughed.
She asked her husband. He laughed.
The both of them laughed. What on earth
Was that woman thinking?
They made love that night. It was fun.
But that was the second use of the penis.

What was the third use of the penis?
Eventually the question became
Kind of a parlor game
For Ann and her circle of friends, of whom
I am lucky enough to count myself one.
That question has happily filled
Many lulls in late-night conversation.
Over the years, we have proposed
Towel rack, swizzle stick, emergency fish bait.
Nothing seems exactly right.
Any man who goes off to the john
Is apt to be asked on his return
If he can answer that woman's question.
Nobody can. The question's a joke
But has also become a kind of *koan*.
Many of us, when we're alone—
Washing the dishes, out hunting grouse—
Ask ourselves (and we're serious):
What is the third use of the penis?

Having failed for years, having broken their heads,
Having had laughter but no *satori*,
Ann and her friends have chosen me
To disseminate this mystery.
So I send out the question about the third use
Beyond these friends, this neighborhood,
Out of town and out of state,
To rapists and to feminists,
To homos and to whores,
To men's groups and the motorbike gangs,
To doctors and philosophers, to honeymoon lovers
And couples stuck in counselors' rooms,
To old men fishing in wooden rowboats,
To widows knitting socks and afghans,
To those alone and those with mates,
This question, good to think upon,
A mystery that puzzles, teases, pleases:
What is the third use of the penis?

THE COLD

You've swallowed a wool sock, and you've got
A little sunburn, slight concussion, no big deal.
Too healthy for the hospital, too sick for work.
Stay home, then. Catch up on your dreams—
The special technicolor vehicles with Dolby stereo
And the black-and-white classics in which you can't speak.
Are you awake? Right. Now what? Breakfast.
Now what? Rest. Read. Abuse yourself. Was that fun?
You could try the TV. You haven't missed a thing:
Jennifer and Lance are still stuck on each other,
Despite the operation, despite the abortion, despite
Her kleptomania, the murder he committed, they're still mad
About each other, still the same cute couple.
What day is this? You yawn. Involuntary tears
Slide out of your eyes and into your ears.
They don't mean a thing. You're just feeling
Sorry for yourself. That's what's wrong with you, you
Never cared about anyone but you, and you
Didn't even do that very well. Well,
You could write to your Aunt Margaret.
She's always been so nice to you, you only owe her
Several billion letters, and you're not so sick
That you can't hold a pen. Dear Aunt Maggie,
But what can you say? Nothing ever happens
To you, you've never been to Africa, never
Seen a single movie star, you've had this stupid cold
For your entire life. God bless you! What day is this?
If only your dead mom would take your temperature,
If only she'd rest her cool hand on your forehead.
If only your dead dad would bring you some ice cream,
Some seven-up, some orange juice. You never loved them
Half enough, that's what's wrong with you. Admit it.
You're a monster. You've got a mild face, but
Your best friend in high school was gay, leather boots

Excite you, you've got a real sadistic streak,
You'd like to own slaves, your fantasies alone
May well have brought about the women's movement,
You could probably do things to children.
God bless you! You should take an aspirin.
You should change your life. Why do you suppose
They call a cold a cold? It's not. It's hot.
Hot, hot, hot. You've got a runny nose. You're a spoiled brat.
At least you could have paid for Jennifer's abortion.
You could have helped Lance locate a halfway decent lawyer.
Are you crazy? What day is this? How about
A nice hot bath? Get dressed, wash your face,
Or you'll go straight to hell, and you know, now,
What the undergloom is like: glaring lights,
The bargain basement of a large department store,
And the place reserved for you is in Appliances,
Where a thousand color TV sets are tuned
To Lance and Jennifer, turned up really loud.
Your feet will be nailed to the floor,
You'll be forced to watch and listen as the days
Of their lives repeat themselves, as the world turns
On and on, and teenagers across the way turn on
The automatic organ that plays calypso melodies,
Country western, polkas, and Hawaiian wedding music
All at once. What? You don't want that? All right, then.
Do you promise to quit smoking? Do you
Promise to quit drinking? Do you promise
To quit lusting after people you can't have? You can't?
What's wrong with you? You're so stinking weak.
You should make some chicken soup.
You should change your life, because
What you're feeling now isn't half as interesting
As heart disease or love or emphysema, but still
It ought to help you realize: Your days are numbered, baby,
And someday, baby, your number will come up. The man
Who owns the furniture store will show you the shop
He runs next door, where he keeps the knife and the make-up kit,

And he'll fix you a smile that won't quite fit.
Are you comfy? Need your pillows plumped?
You're not really such an awful person,
For a human being. You haven't killed yourself
Yet, and you've worked hard, you've tried.
So go a little easy on yourself. Relax. Don't get up,
Not yet. Because I hate to think how this will end.
You'll get over me, I know. You'll get up and leave me
The same as you left all those others. You'll pretend
This never happened. But I've loved you, nonetheless.
God bless you! My goodness. *God bless you!*

ICEHOUSE

The icehouses lie scattered
Like building blocks some kid
Has kicked across the floor. But no,
As you come closer, crunching through the snow,
You see these are the houses of the poor,
The plywood shacks of shantytown
You never visited before. Here
Fishermen survive on sandwiches,
Candy bars, and beer. Each year
The paper prints hot rumors
Of elusive icehouse whores,
But the truth is disappointing, dull:
There are no mermaids anywhere,
In this world or the other, and this is
A man's world, each black shack
A throwback to the clubhouse
That wore the words No Girls.

These huts are like the houses
Children draw, simple and efficient:
A door, a tiny window, smoke
Escaping in a scribble from the chimney.
Above the door of this one
The fisherman has written
His license, name, and his address—
Orville Sundquist, 37 Acorn Street,
Esko, Minnesota—as if his blackhouse
Were a package that contained
The man he always meant to be
And he hoped that somehow somebody
Would finally mail him home.

Inside, Orville, who is huge,
Hunches on a little stool

And jigs a mini fishing pole.
The stove that heats his house is small,
The sticks he feeds it kindling. Here
In his cramped confessional
Orville contemplates the zero
That his life has come to, skims
The crust that clouds the hole,
Reopening the wound, and meditates
On might-have-beens, evaporating dreams:
Christine, a degree in forestry,
That bass boat with the Evinrude
He'll never own. Well, maybe
Once the kids are grown.

The wind comes up, and Orville
Thinks of heading home. But then
He feels a signal from below
And hauls from out the icy hole
A shining thing, green-gold, glittering,
With fins, an alligator nose,
And eyes that glaze but cannot close.

A LITTLE LITANY FOR MOVING DAY

The woman who packs up the kitchen
Sees how the silver has blackened.
She wraps the crystal in newsprint
From which the stories are fading.

The man who wrestles mattresses
Understands love is ambiguous,
Dreams are both good and bad,
The truth is too large to embrace.

> *Thus I renounce the illusion of ownership;*
> *Thus I renounce the things of this world.*
> *I am not my belongings;*
> *Neither do things own my soul.*

The easy chair is tired.
The floor lamp gives no light.
Books that once were bright with life
Are dark and dead as bricks.

Papa has been put to rest.
He is not this chest of drawers.
Mama will be dead forever.
What are these snapshots for?

> *Thus I renounce the illusion of ownership;*
> *Thus I renounce the things of this world.*
> *I am not my belongings;*
> *Neither do things own my soul.*

The fewer things that we possess
The less we are possessed.
Birds migrate twice a year
And like to build new nests.

Horrified, the baby cries:
"What are you going to do?
Don't take down my bed!"
But by-and-by
Everything and all of us
Will have to go
Bye-bye.

TACONITE HARBOR

The houses stand still, but the people are gone,
As if somebody had dropped a neutron bomb.
The families who lived here put their trust
In a company that cared about money alone.
They called these look-alike houses home,
A lie that lasted till the mine went bust.
How could an entire town be so naive?
You shake your head in disbelief,
Note the scrawny trees that cast no shade,
The asphalt streets where children played,
The overgrown gardens, the scruffy lawns,
The way the picture windows seem to yawn.
There was never a church, a school, or a store,
And nobody has lived here in a year or more.
Some houses will be moved, the rest torn down.
No one ever lived here. There's no such town.

MY FATHER AT HIS HEIGHT

I grew to his exact same size,
But I'll never be half as handsome
As he was that June afternoon
I remember (wrongly, no doubt)
As the absolute prime of his life:
Five or six minutes at a Bible camp
On the banks of the Rainy River.
He's thirty back there, maybe thirty-two,
And we stand on the splintery dock
Where he's guarding the lives
Of two dozen loud adolescents.
The river is wide as the world
To me, cold and deep, dark blue.
He stands just short of five feet eight—
The same as I do today—
But I am quite small in memory,
And my father seems very tall.
His legs are strong and hairy,
His chest is smooth and brown,
His bathing trunks are navy blue.
A silver whistle on a leather thong
Hangs loosely around his neck.
He smiles down and tells me
We're going to be moving soon.
He has put in his name for a call
And already written one parish
To say if they want anyone good at all
They'll have to offer more money than that.
Such confidence! He'll never
Be so decisive again. I remember
Him flying out of the pulpit
And hauling me down through the nave
Because I had misbehaved; I remember
His silk soft robes, as white

As the wings of a vengeful angel.
And later, once, his great disgust
When his wife was dying and the president
Of the bank called out in front of everyone:
"Hey, Sutter! Do you know you're overdrawn?"
But mostly, there was the man
So passive he wouldn't change
Channels on the TV. In this picture, though,
He is proud and young and understands
Women, cars, the Holy Ghost, everything
I don't. He knows Indians in Canada
Who've told him where to pick berries.
And the customs men at the border
Wave him on through, they know him,
Everyone knows him, they call him
Pastor or Reverend. He shouts
At one of the swimmers: "Come back!
Don't go so far out!" Here in midlife,
I wonder what that young man wants
And guess: minor, local importance;
To baptize, marry, and bury;
To sing some old songs about Jesus;
To make love with his wife at night
(All to the glory of God, of course);
A decent salary; a future
For me and my baby brother; a cabin
On a lake. But life is a river
And flows in ways he can't predict.
His wife will go rotten with cancer
And die, his children will not believe
In his God, he will be horribly unhappy
But smile and call this God's will, whatever
Happens to happen. And I realize now,
Way too late, that this fellow,
My father, both gentle and hard,
Is a terrifying young man,
Because he believes in Jesus,

Someone he's never seen;
Because he believes what he does
Is God's will, and his God
Is foggier than a cloud; he believes
In the Holy Spirit, who is less real
Than the wind that stirs the green reeds
In the river. What he loves in his heart
Of hearts can't be seen, and none of this,
None of us—the squealing kids in the water,
The screams of his wife in her agony,
This moment passing between us,
The yellow smell of the sunlight—
None of this really matters.
Now he is over seventy, weak,
His body dragged down by gravity,
Losing his sight and his memories,
And for all of his talk about heaven,
He is scared to death of dying.
But not back here in this memory,
Which isn't his but mine. Back here
He is terribly stupid and brave,
He rests a hand on my head like a blessing,
Blows the bright whistle, and shouts:
"All right! That's it! Everyone out of the water!"

GEORGE

Didn't own much
But forty acres of popple and hay,
A shack of a house,
A swaybacked barn,
A Model T
That wouldn't drive,
An Allis Chalmers
Needed parts.
Why did he live that way?
Not that he wasn't smart.
A backwoods, radical Democrat,
Debated with my dad,
A timid, village Republican
Who swore George must be nuts
But liked him all the more.
George argued hot
But laughed a lot.
Had a goony grin
With missing teeth,
A smell like sour milk
And smoke. I was five
And afraid of him,
But I liked his jokes,
His bony cows,
His ugly face and clothes.
Had a railroad cap
And overalls,
A blue bandana,
Filthy boots. A skinny,
Wiry, scarecrow guy.
A man like a piece of wood.

To go see George
You'd walk the plank

He'd dropped across the ditch,
Wade through daisies, tiger lilies
Up to his drooping porch.
Buster came to lick your hand,
And George yelled out hello.
Had a mail-order bride
From the Ozark hills,
Soft and fat and fine.
A cripple, Bertha
Hollered hi,
Wheeled around, jammed
Three chunks in the red-hot stove,
And slammed the lid on yellow flames.
She was a laugher, too,
And all the time
She used to go, "Oh, George."
George was the one
Who cut her the wood,
He was the man with the saw.
Hauled her water in metal pails
And carried out the slops.
Did they make love? Well,
I can't say, but he made her laugh
As if.

I stayed with them,
And they were strange:
Scraped my skin with gritty soap,
Put butter on my eggs,
Used branches off the trees for brooms,
And slept in the living room.
They gave me threadbare spools
For toys. Bertha painted
California, Florida—
Rocky cliffs and gleaming seas,
The flashing fins of sharks.
After supper the room grew dim.
We sat there in the dark.

What didn't they own, those two?
No kids, no toilet, no TV.
They had the dog for company.
No fancy pants, no cocktail dress,
One set of Sunday clothes.
No shining crystal dining room
But a table out under the trees.
No telephone, no radio.
Breeze in the aspen leaves.

Once, at sunset, driving past,
My father said, "Look there."
And there was George, hands on hips,
Standing on a stack of hay,
Staring into the sun that blazed
Bright as a large gold coin.
"George is a dreamer," my father said.
"George is plenty deep." And out of respect,
He drove on by and didn't honk hello.

My father told me George had said
That he'd seen Jesus once.
Woke in the night, and there He was,
Right at the foot of his bed.
George couldn't tell
What the Lord looked like
Because He was a great white light,
But the Master told him, "I say unto thee:
Rich men make my body bleed.
Be poor and follow me."

MRS.

What I'd really like to do tonight
Is go downstairs and sit with Mrs.
Court. Knock three times and enter
When her cracked voice croaks out, "Come!"
Clear the cluttered sofa, sit
Beside seed catalogues, the Monkey Wards
Wish book, her heavy German Bible.
Imbibe a beer or coffee, nibble cookies,
Praise her latest quilt. I'll tell her
Gory details of the accident
I witnessed last time I was in the Cities.
She'll be thrilled and glad she's living
Where she'll die, Stearns County.
We'll watch a hockey game or dream
The green of next year's garden,
Get her going on the days back when
She worked from dark to dark—
Canning, baking, making hay,
Minding kids and mending clothes.
Tonight's the night she'll tell us
Of the dreamhouse that she never dared
Tell anyone about but us—
Round and stone, unburnable,
Pure fantasy, a wish as pure
As her belief in God. And then
My wife and the old lady, women
Forty years apart, will start in
On their most amusing subject, men.
I'll grin and egg them on
Till Mrs. Court says, smiling slyly,
"I know men. I had one of my own,
You know." "We know," we'll nod,
Although we never met the man.

"When I and Pete got married
We didn't have a penny," she'll begin,
And she'll be gone, newlywed again,
Working in the fields beside her husband.
She'll give birth to children, raise them up,
And love them, though she'll never say so.
"Love," she'll scoff. "Now there's a word
You hear on television. I and Pete, we never,
Well, you just never used it!
You had the kids, you fed them good,
You made their clothes, my goodness,
You looked *after* them, and when you couldn't
Do for them the way you wanted to,
You felt bad. What else is there?"
Silence. We won't know what to answer.
So she'll go back to Pete. I and Pete,
I and Pete, a phrase that she'll repeat
Like a pattern in her fancywork.
She'll tell us how the man made
Homebrew in the barn during Prohibition
And sold it at the Rockville dance.
How he was big. How he could eat!
How he grew tons of onions,
Flagged his neighbors down,
And forced them to accept his aromatic gifts.
How he was crazy over horses,
Hated tractors, and when he finally bought one
How he drove it in the ditch,
Pulling on the steering wheel and shouting, "Whoa!"
She'll keep his memory alive by laughing at him.
The name beside her number in the phone book
Won't be hers but his. And the brass crucifix
She snatched off his casket at the funeral
Will be fastened to the wall. Her own name,
Magdalena, is majestic, archangelic,
But we'll respect her wishes
And never call her anything but Mrs.

To go downstairs and sit with her
Would be some kind of fun,
But Mrs. Court was taken to the nursing home,
Her foot removed by surgeons
Who later took her leg. Diabetes.
Something that the three of us had joked about.
She lay there like a snowdrift in her bed
When we finally visited. She didn't know us
But twisted round and looked at us
Like a dog who'd been hit by a truck
But hadn't died just yet. We stood
Above her bed and sweated, nervous,
Trembling, stammering for words
Our college educations hadn't taught us.
Her eyes were wet, black stones,
And we spoke to her at last as though
We were speaking down into a well.
"Thank you for those funny stories."
"And thanks for that quilt. We still use it."
"You should see the garden we've got now—
Beets, beans, tomatoes, scads of onions."
"I'm sorry that you can't remember us."
"You were always a very good neighbor."
Simple stuff. Country talk.
Nothing worked. Nothing brought her back
Until we mentioned Pete and named her kids.
"Has Dominic been here? How's Peggy?
And Theresa?" Then she smiled weakly,
Grimacing, announcing in her skinny voice,
"They're fine. Everybody's fine."
"Can we get you anything?"
"I've got everything I need."

We were nobody she knew.
There was nothing we could do
For her, and so we drove away
Through stunted, withered fields,

A mirage of water on the road
Receding like the hope of rain
That summer, a bad one for the farmers.

WHY BIRCH TREES ARE WHITE

I've seen thousands, millions by now, and still they amaze me. On hot, sticky days their trunks remind me of columns of snow, and the green froth of their foliage is also refreshing. In winter they fit with the snowscape or stand out from the boring background of popple and brush like those people at parties you want to meet right away.

Birches were to the Ojibway what buffalo were to the Sioux. They used them for wigwams, baskets, canoes ... Those trees are still with us, but look at the poor buffalo. Slaughtered by whites by the millions. Buffalo traveled in gigantic herds and raised a real ruckus, not to mention the dust. But birches were too tough to eat, and they didn't make such a fuss. They kept quiet and stayed in one place. There might be a lesson in that. Even though the giant red and white pines have gone the way of the buffalo, where the softwoods were felled birches grew up and still flourish, touch wood.

But why are they white? And why am I so glad to see them? It must have something to do with the snow. Perhaps it's protective coloration. After all, it's winter here seven months out of the year. When the weather gets cold the ptarmigan turns white, and so does the snowshoe hare. Think of polar bears. And the Finns, in World War II, they only had rifles and skis, but they dressed in white clothes, and they held off the whole Russian army for weeks. So maybe that's why birch trees are white.

But why am I so glad to see them? I don't understand it, but birch trees are kind of like women to me: they make me excited and peaceful. When I drive past a stand of birches, it's as if I'm driving by a hospital just as a whole flock of nurses are getting off work. I look and look. And all of these wonderful women I see, they don't care about me, but they make me feel lucky to be here. If you get up close to a birch tree you notice the bark isn't white after all but silver, pale green, pink and blue. Nothing is simple, neither peace nor love nor the color of birch trees. As I write these words down on white paper, paper made out of wood, Finland is peaceful, Russia is calling its armies home, Sweden is peaceful, Norway, Denmark, the States, Canada, the entire domain of the birch is at peace. And if you stretch out under a birch with someone you love—or even someone you like a little—you can feel, for a minute or two, the great calm under all things, the peace so profound it passes all understanding.

FISHING AT FORTY

for Louis Jenkins

We got ourselves up
For one last trip, gathered our gear,
Kissed the women goodbye, and drove
A hundred miles under smoldering skies.
Decorated with yellow leaves,
The lake was a mosaic of reflections
Where we drifted, casting this way and that,
Like someone searching his mind for an answer.

What was it you wanted
Back there in your twenties?
A woman writhing and moaning your name?
The nod and good word of a man you admired?
Wishes and dreams had come to pass,
And still you felt like a failure.
The woods had promised visions once,
But what you got was what was there:
Spiced air and silence, mist on the water ...
You got what you brought: sausage and cheese,
Your own foggy thoughts, passing
Brandy around the fire. And what was left,
What had you saved for your later years?
The consolation of memories? Insomnia? Disease?
You might still put together some words
That would last. But aging meant gradually giving up
All you loved best: tobacco and liquor,
Reading and sex. In the end, in the home, you'd refuse
Even food, groaning and waving the tray away.

I caught one fish, a small rainbow,
And held him high for my pal to admire.
The shimmer, the sheen, the shine of a trout!

Then rain dotted down. We made for shore,
Where I gutted the fish, tore out his gills,
And left the red mess for the coons to devour.
What next? Nothing to do but drive
The back roads, pull at the whiskey,
Stare through the rain, and wish it would quit.
Car-fishing, we called it.
You didn't catch much, but you didn't get wet.
We nosed through the bush, jounced over rocks,
Swerved around deadfalls, splashed
Through mudholes, planning, complaining ...
The lake we wanted never appeared.
We took the wrong roads,
Misread the map, and just like that
Our season was over. The rain had eased off,
But the daylight was gone. We found
The highway and turned toward home. Wind
Whipped wet leaves through the headlights.
The branches of birches flashed by
Like lightning. Quick as a thought,
A coyote shot across the road and into the woods.
So a man over forty thinks of his death—
Quickly, several times each day.
My friend groaned out
The words to a song about "easy lovin',"
Though he knew it wasn't. Weary,
We wondered whether the trip had been worth it.
I thought of my rainbow back in the cooler,
Already losing his pinks and blues,
His silver and steel; the whiskey
Behind the seat, half gone;
The long, hard winter coming on.

THE FIRST HARD FROST

The radio predicts the first hard frost,
And so I hurry home, speeding north for hours,
Knowing my wife will be gone, the garden ruined,
Green things blackened by the blowtorch of the cold
Unless I rescue them. But when I check
Our co-op garden plot, the ground is bare.
Shocked, I wonder who and think of teenage vandals,
But when I drive around to the apartment
There's a sack of green tomatoes in the hall,
And, opening the door, I walk into a wedding.
Flowers everywhere. Bachelor buttons in a cup.
Roses in a glass. Cosmos in a copper vase—
Orange, pink, purple, white—surrounded by their greens.
And there's another bunch like fireworks,
Exploding from an aqua mason jar.
On the table, a note from my wife
Says goodbye and mentions love,
Calls me dear and says enjoy the roses,
Roses she has stolen from the city garden,
The last, the final roses from that garden,
Soon to be demolished for a freeway.
We had roses at our wedding, but those were only yellow,
Whereas these are red and pink and bruised,
Spotted here and there with dots of brown
Like the hands of men and women who have aged.
In the bathroom there's a bud beheaded in a bowl,
The bedroom blooms with roses red and white.
I stand in the living room and laugh
At this extravagant profusion, dizzied
By the crazy colors, breathing rich perfume.

But I've got work to do, and so I crack the black anthology,
Turning to the story I've assigned my students,
And have to laugh again because I've picked "A Rose

For Emily." In Faulkner's awful story, Emily
Is so in love with Homer she'd rather have him dead
Than let him go. The entire town is just about to learn
She's kept his carcass in her bed when my neighbor calls
To let me know her husband's in the hospital.
"I'll be right down," I say, and go. She pours out
Her troubles with our coffee. "Last night
He backed me up against the wall. He hurt me.
Clayton!" Her arms are badly bruised.
"What else could I do? He was after me!"
Her fingers fidget with the filigree
Embroidered on the tablecloth. I take her hand
And tell her she did right. Nearly eighty now,
She's small and fierce, half deaf,
Her bad eyes magnified by heavy glasses.
Grandma Italy, we call her, although her name is Grace.
She's cared for Clayton these last years,
Refusing to let go, though he's become robotic,
Stiff and scary, frozen by the strokes.
But now the end has come. We know it.
A sob escapes her twisted lips. "Oh, why
Does it have to be this way?"
She says, "God!" Then glares at me and snarls,
"Who said these were the golden years?"

I climb the stairs and think of taking her
Some flowers—she's a green-thumb gardener—
But then forget, my thoughts on Clayton,
So frightening because he couldn't smile,
Spoke in moans, sat rigid in his easy chair
For hours, like some astronaut we'd lost.
Grace has called him "Honey" to the last,
Insisting "He was always such a helpful man,"
Recalling how he whistled all day long,
Told tongue-twisters to children,
And walked downtown in a smart silk suit,
Straw hat on his head, carnation stuck in his lapel.

He will die now, any day. We know it.
They'll have flowers at his funeral because
We mark the things that matter—birth and death
And marriage—with all kinds of flowers,
Though roses are preferred. And I know
That once the snow retreats, Grace will be out
In the yard, in a pink housedress and a man's straw hat,
Kneeling in her flowerbeds, tending to her peonies,
Handling the tiny seeds that she can hardly see,
Nursing the nasturtiums, the pansies, the cosmos.

I can almost see her down there now,
As if the dark were day, as if the month were May,
And I lift a rose like a glass of wine
And breathe the deep, dark odor of the stolen flower,
A strange perfume that mingles mint
With the smoky scent of sex, something sweet
With something earthy underneath, a dark, ripe
Odor like the dark bouquet of dark red wine,
The purple fragrance of a burgundy or cabernet,
Wine so dark it's like a glass of night.

DRIFTROSE

What weird rewards the waves wash up.
There we sat, still married, but only just barely,
Softer than water, harder than rocks,
Perched on boulders as big as our bodies.
The horizon was empty except for one salty
Sailing for someplace we'd never go.
You talked about moving. I walked off and wept,
Returned, ran my hand all over your back.
Driftwood and pebbles, the catcalls of gulls.
We talked about the house, how much to ask,
All those things I couldn't pay back.
And suddenly you dipped up out of the slosh
A single, drifting, long-stemmed rose.
Who knows where love comes from or where it goes?
There are thousands of things I can't understand,
Including that wet rose you held in your hand.

WIFE

Oh, my old darling, my dear one, my friend,
I can't believe we've come to this end.

You—whom I've loved so badly so long,
For whom I was unable to break into song—

Gave me money and love, but, sick with greed,
I've somehow decided that's not what I need.

Oh, my old darling, my dear one, my friend,
I can't believe I've brought on this end.

We were prudent, quite careful. We took our time.
We'd seen how marriages got undermined.

We were so smart, with all our degrees,
We swore we'd do things differently.

Oh, my old darling, my dear one, my friend,
Who would have thought we'd come to this end?

I see you at twenty, striding down the street
In your navy pea coat, brave and petite,

And later, in Paris, naked in bed,
Grinning and waving a long loaf of bread.

Oh, my old darling, my dear one, my friend,
Maybe this isn't really the end

But some new beginning. We might make this work
If I could quit being such a damn jerk,

If you could find the panther inside you,
If I could let go, come out of hiding.

Oh, my old darling, it's useless, my friend,
To think we can fix this, put off the end.

I can blame it on Mother, or maybe my dad,
Or call myself rotten, awful, and bad,

But marriages fail, and this one is dead.
Someone will love you far more than I did.

Oh, my old darling, my dear one, sweet friend,
I am so sorry we've come to this end.

THE WORK

The work, which no one asked me to do,
For which there is little demand,
Grows lonelier as I get older. All these years
And I'm still sitting here at the desk.
The night gets larger and the lamp grows dim.
More and more often I ask:
What for? How come? People hate poems.
What is all this, anyway, this
Doodling in the face of death, some
Sort of ancestor worship? To whom
Do I owe all these letters
And when will those creatures write back?
Do I think I'm leaving messages
For the inhabitants of Pluto?
As of this writing, 250,000
Humans are born every day.
The missiles are poised, bombers
Drift through the heavens,
The submarines play hide-and-seek.
Rain will erase every tombstone,
And yet we hire stonecutters
To carve the names of the missing in granite,
Adding, perhaps, a small poem.
How can we be so dumb?
Where is it we learn
Even things not worth doing
Are worth doing well?
I rip the page from the tablet
And start all over again.

Acknowledgments

Thanks to Annette Atkins, John Engman, David Jauss, and Louis Jenkins, who helped me improve many of the new poems in this collection.

Cedarhome was published by BOA Editions in 1977. *Pine Creek Parish Hall and Other Poems* was published by Sandhills Press in 1985 and reissued by Greysolon Press in 1990.

Of the new poems in this collection, "The Cold" and "The Third Use of the Penis" appeared in *North Coast Review,* "A Little Litany for Moving Day" in *North Dakota Quarterly,* and "Fishing at Forty" in *The Chariton Review.*

A number of these poems were staged as *Small Town Triumphs* at the Great American History Theatre of St. Paul in April and May of 1992.

I am grateful for a Loft-McKnight Award and a Bush Artist Fellowship, both of which allowed me to complete some of these poems.

—Barton Sutter

A Note About the Author

Born in Minneapolis in 1949, Barton Sutter was raised in small towns in Minnesota and Iowa. He attended Bemidji State, Southwest State, and Syracuse University. For ten years he worked as a typesetter; more recently he has earned his living as a free-lance writer and teacher. Barton Sutter has adapted his poetry for the stage, he has published a collection of stories called *My Father's War,* and he writes a monthly essay for Minnesota Public Radio. The recipient of several awards—including the Bassine Citation from The Academy of American Poets, a Loft-McKnight Award, and a Bush Foundation Fellowship—he lives in Duluth, Minnesota.

BOA EDITIONS, LTD.
AMERICAN POETS CONTINUUM SERIES

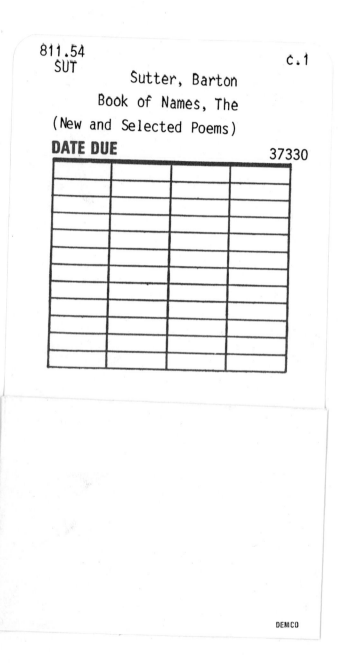